The
Heartsong
Tofu
Cookbook

The Heartsong Tofu Cookbook

Recipes by Toni Heartsong

Instructions on tofu making ~ Bob Heartsong

Banyan Books
Miami, Fla.

Revised edition 1978
Third printing   1978

Designed and hand lettered by the authors.
Manufactured in the United States of America.

ISBN 0-916224-16-3

For those beings who have
the will to discover the truth
and the imagination to
create with it.

Table of Contents

We would like to introduce to you ~ TOFU! ~ the magical soybean product that has changed our lives and has made meal time in our home a unique and delicious adventure!

"The Soybean"~

One of natures highest sources of protein transformed into delicate curds, so versatile it can replace meat, cheese and eggs in texture, flavor, and nutrition!

America grows more soybeans than anywhere else in the world and the majority of them are either fed to cattle or made into plastic! Yet, the soybean is the potential answer to the world food shortage. It is a source of the finest protein man can assimilate.

People get so bored eating the same things day after day, always looking for something new and different. Tofu is it! It is inexpensive, healthy, easy to prepare, versatile and delicious! After many months of working with tofu I am convinced the possibilities are endless.

I hope this book will be a source of imaginative cooking ideas for you. It is not intended to teach you how to cook, but to combine your talent and imagination using tofu. These recipes can be intensified or changed ... don't be afraid to explore, as tofu is so easy to work with, quite truthfully, everything I make comes out a taste treat! There are no mistakes ~ just good food and fun!

Yoni Heartsong

8

Tofu Is Good for You

The soybean has played such an important role in protein sources for hundreds of years in China and Japan. During our present day food crisis, the waste of our farm land is an outrage. Growing soybeans could produce 33% more protein per acre than the same use of the land to grow feed for beef cattle. It is time for America to wake up to the fact that without a drastic change in our consciousness, the future of mankind will look very grim. I know it is difficult for many of us to give up the idea of a carnivorous diet, our taste buds and education have been so programmed but let me tell you about the qualities of soybeans + tofu and perhaps together we can work to make our planet healthy and free of disease and hunger.

Soybeans contain about 35% protein, all 8 essential amino acids, no cholesterol and almost no saturated fats. It is the perfect diet food with 8 ounces containing 147 calories.

The American diet with high amounts of saturated fats and cholesterol has produced a nation of very unhealthy people. Chemicals, processed foods, diets that depend on meat, sugar, eggs and dairy have resulted in an unbelievable rate of heart disease, cancer, circulatory disease and mental illness. In China, heart disease is no problem by comparison. The Hunzas are famous for their long life. Animal products make up 1½% of their total diet. Americans use 70% animal products in their diet. It is interesting to note that the vegetarians are 20 pounds below the national average weight.

An 8 oz. serving of tofu supplies 11.5 grams of usable protein ~ 27% of the daily adult male protein requirement.

Tofu contains lecithin which helps break up fats in the body. 8 oz. provides 38% of the daily requirement of calcium. It is rich in minerals: iron, phosphorus potassium, sodium, essential B vitamins, choline and vitamin E.

Tofu is alkaline. Japanese doctors recommend it for diabetes, heart trouble, hardening of the arteries, and circulatory difficulties.

Some proteins are rather difficult to assimilate, but tofu is easily digested. Because of its unique process which removes the crude-fiber and water soluable carbohydrates from the soybean, it is transformed into a soft, highly digestible food. (95% digestible)

Whole cooked soybeans are 68% digestible. Even babies can enjoy tofu!

It is easy to see that tofu is beneficial to the young and old!

It is low in cost, too! If homemade, a serving will cost about 6½ ¢.

Tofu is so delicious when prepared in your favorite recipes, it can truly be stated that tofu has the potential of reversing the disease statistics to help the world bring about a total rebirthing!

13

Okara
"honorable shell"

Okara contains important "dietary plant fiber" which is considered a must in every well-balanced diet. Fiber has two main functions ~ It provides bulk (roughage) necessary for regular bowel movements, and it absorbs toxins, such as environmental pollutants, and speeds their passage out of the body.

Okara contains approximately 17% protein in the original soybean. 3.5 by weight, or about the same proportion found in whole milk or cooked brown rice.

Using the okara is just as important as using the tofu, and this by-product can be used in so many different recipes!

I Make Tofu

& instructions

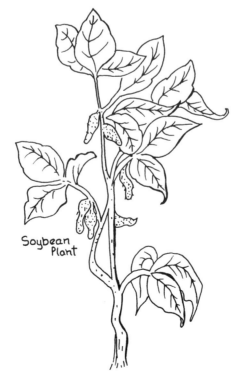

Soybean
Plant

I Make Tofu !

Making tofu is not very difficult. An hour or two of time, a few pieces of equipment, your love and rapt attention and you will have several delicious meals made from your own tofu. A delight!

2000 years ago a gentle Chinese soul stumbled into the way of tofu. For two thousand or more years tofu has been a staple on Oriental tables. Tofu is old – yet it is being renewed. Here in the West the way of tofu has just begun – and you need only your imagination and a cube of tofu to take the first step.

I Make Tofu !

Ingredients:
- 1½ cups large cooking soybeans
- 16 cups pure water
- 2 teaspoons Nigari, Epsom salts or calcium sulfate (gypsum)

or

- ¼ cup lemon juice or apple cider vinegar

Utensils:
- 2½ gallon pot
- 2 qt. saucepan
- Rice paddle
- Large strainer
- Ladle
- Large pot to catch soymilk
- Metal colander
- Measuring spoons
- Pressing Sack ~(Can be made from sewn together cotton diapers, a pillow case or any cotton material which is suitable)
- Cheese cloth
- Blender
- Potato masher or jar
- Settling box

17

Suggested Equipment

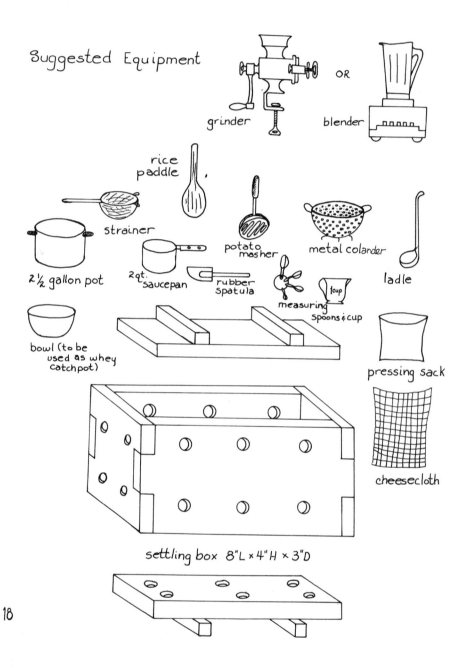

grinder   OR   blender

rice paddle

strainer

2 ½ gallon pot

2 qt. saucepan

potato masher

rubber spatula

metal colander

measuring spoons & cup

ladle

bowl (to be used as whey catchpot)

pressing sack

cheesecloth

settling box   8"L × 4"H × 3"D

18

Procedure

Wash and soak soybeans for 8 to 10 hours prior to making tofu ~ longer if the temperature is below 60°. Rinse beans again before using.

Prepare in advance ~ Lay open pressing sack in colander. Set colander in milk catch pot. Lay cheese cloth in settling box and set atop pot or bowl as to catch excess whey.

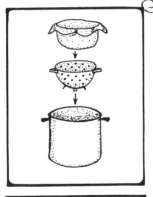

19

I. Heat 11½ cups water in large pot (a). On another burner heat 3 cups water in pot (b) over low heat. Preheat blender with hot tap water to prevent cracking, then put ½ Soaked beans in blender with 2½ cups of hot water from large pot (a). Blend until smooth puree (2-3 minutes in blender). While blending remove 2½ more cups hot water from pot (a). Pour puree in hot water pot (a). Puree remaining beans and water and add to pot.

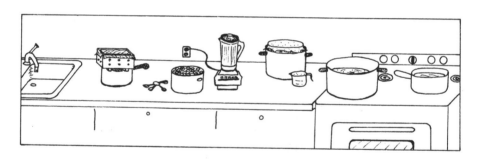

II. Stir constantly to prevent sticking and burning. Bring to boil~ When pot foams up rapidly, turn off burner and stir foam down. Pour contents of pot into pressing sack~slowly!

III. Twist sack closed and press against side of colander. with masher or jar until most of milk is extracted. Open mouth of sack, pour 3 cups water from pot (b) over *okara. Close sack and press again.

   *Save Okara.

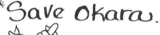

IV. Pour soymilk into clean, large pot (a) and bring to boil. Stir bottom occasionally ~ Simmer for 5 to 7 minutes. While simmering, add solidifier to 1 cup warm water and dissolve. Turn off burner and add 1/3 solidifier by stirring pot clockwise, stopping paddle abruptly in pot and pouring solidifier down side of paddle, where pocket forms (this may take some practice). Stir briskly back and forth, 4 strokes. Add second third of solidifier by sprinkling over surface of soymilk. Cover and allow to stand for 3-5 minutes. Uncover and sprinkle last third of solidifier over surface while stirring upper inch of soymilk gently until white curds separate from yellow whey. If milkiness remains add 1/4 teaspoon of solidifier into 1/4 cup warm water and stir into pot gently.

22

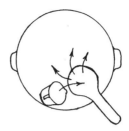

V. When curds and whey have separated, place strainer in pot and ladle out whey. Scoop out curds and gently place them in settling box until all are in box. Cover with cheesecloth, put lid on and press with 1 pound weight for 15 minutes ~ longer for firmer tofu. Take weight off, remove lid and immerse tofu in cold water for 3 minutes. Unwrap cheesecloth and prepare to serve or cut and store in covered container filled with water. Refrigerate.

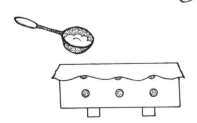
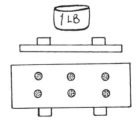

1 LB

Change water daily...
   Can be stored for 5 to 7 days.

Use whey for washing pots, as
a soup base or watering plants!

24

Recipes

I. Tofu Main Dishes

Stir-Fried Tofu
~with Vegies~

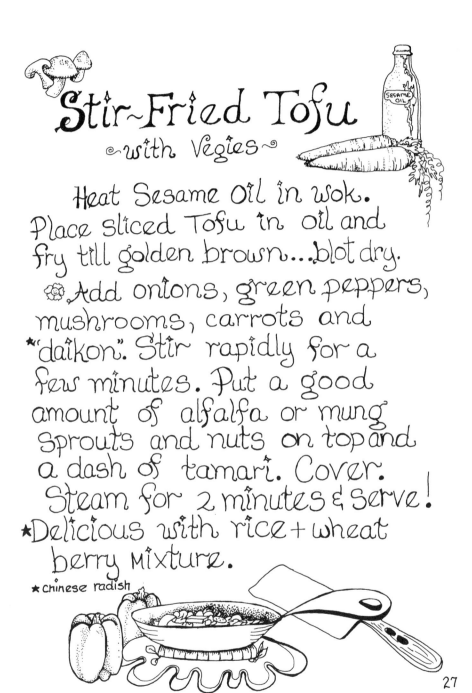

Heat Sesame Oil in wok. Place sliced Tofu in oil and fry till golden brown...blot dry.

Add onions, green peppers, mushrooms, carrots and *"daikon". Stir rapidly for a few minutes. Put a good amount of alfalfa or mung sprouts and nuts on top and a dash of tamari. Cover. Steam for 2 minutes & serve!

*Delicious with rice + wheat berry mixture.

*chinese radish

27

Broiled Tofu

Use marinade recipe given ~
(Over night)

Slice tofu in large pieces.
Place on broiler pan. Sprinkle
with paprika. Broil on both
sides till browned.

Sauté vegetables-place on top of
tofu; a little longer... in the oven ~
and serve!

Broiled Tofu #2

Slice tofu ¼" thin.
Melt *soy margarine in
sauce pan adding garlic
powder and tamari~
Dip tofu in butter mixture
~dust with primary yeast
flakes. Place on broiling
pan and brown.

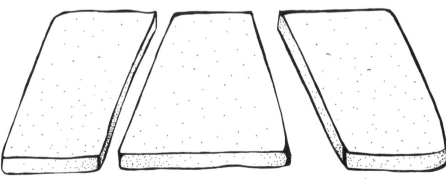

(* Soy margarine or soy butter can be purchased at your local health food store. "Willow Run" is recommended.)

Tofu Tempura

Cut tofu in long strips... heat oil and fry, drain, cool.

Batter: 1 cup chickpea flour
1¼ cup pure water
1 teaspoon curry
garlic

Dip tofu in batter. Put back in oil until crispy. Add other vegetables, if you like!

Serve with
Tofu Dip

Tofu Loaf

4 pieces tofu (20 oz.)
1 cup toasted wheat germ
1 cup whole wheat bread crumbs
1 cup diced onions
1 cup diced peppers
1 cup diced mushrooms
1 cup bean sprouts
½ cup walnuts

Season with tamari, sea salt,
basil, ginger... (to taste)

Sauté vegetables in oil with
¼ t. ginger ~ Add T. tamari.
Pour into mashed tofu with
chopped walnuts. Add seasoning.
Mix together ~ mixture should
be fairly dry. Put into loaf
pan. ~ brush top with tamari.
Bake 35-40 minutes ~ 350°
Do not cover... Serve with
gravy or ketchup ~

31

Vegetarian Tofu Chopped Liver

3 cups chopped onions
1 cup chopped mushrooms
1 cup finely grated carrots
3/4 cup sesame butter
1/4 cup tamari
1 cube tofu (8 oz.) mashed
garlic (to taste)

Sauté onions and mushrooms about 15 minutes in oil ...
Add carrots ~ cooking 5 more minutes. Stir well adding remainder of ingredients~
Cook a few minutes.

Om~Fu 中学

Dice carrots, onions, green pepper, celery.

Crumble Tofu.

Saute vegetables in sesame oil. Add tofu, sesame seeds, parsley ~ tamari and kelp.

CORN~FU

4 ears fresh corn
1 cube tofu (6 oz.)
1 small red onion
3 mushrooms, sliced
¼ stick soy butter

Melt butter in wok, sauté onion. Combine husked corn, crumbled tofu. Cook at medium heat for about 10 minutes. Add sliced mushrooms... Sprinkle with tamari.

34

"Tofu Antoinette"

Melt approx. ½ stick soy butter,
Slice tofu in strips and brown
in wok ~ Add fresh, cut
string beans and sliced yellow
Squash ~ in equal amounts.
Now add garlic, tamari, and
a squeeze of lime juice to suit
your taste –
   Sauté for about 5 minutes ~
and add 1 cup of whole
   wheat bread crumbs, toss
a few more minutes and
      Voilà !!!

Tofu Bulgar Pilaf

1 cup bulgar
2 cups water or stock
3 T. soy margarine
¼ t. basil
8 oz. tofu
1 T. miso
¼ t. ginger (minced)
¼ t. sesame salt
1 minced onion

Melt soy margarine in wok ~ Add bulgar, onions, sauté 5 minutes.
Add water, basil + ginger. Cover and bring to a boil. Reduce heat and simmer until liquid is absorbed (about 15 minutes). Combine tofu and miso in small bowl, mashing together, stir into grain.
Serve with sesame salt.
Top with parsley.

Tofu~Rice Croquettes

4 cups steamed brown rice
4 cups tofu
½ cup peanut butter
2 t. salt
2 T. oil
1 T. onion powder or ¼ cup chopped onion
3 T. tamari
1 cup chopped parsley
~ garlic ~

mix together... add seasoning
to taste and form into patties.
Sprinkle with paprika + sesame
seeds. Bake at 350°, turn
to brown on all sides.
Serve with tofu sauce (recipe given.)

Tofu Casserole

Sauté onions, peppers, mushrooms and slices of tofu. Add garlic, oregano, tarragon.

Cook a pot of brown rice and wheat berries.

Prepare Tofu Sauce
(recipe given)

Combine in casserole dish, layering vegetables, rice + sauce. Top with sunflower seeds and bake.

Tofu ~ Spinach Pie

3 cups marinaded tofu (mashed)
3/4 cup olive oil
1 pound diced onions
1/2 cup chopped, fresh parsley
1/2 cup chopped, fresh dill or
            2 T. dill weed.
1 T. salt... Garlic to taste
3½ cups steamed spinach
Pie crust dough for 1 large pie

Heat oil in wok, add onions, slowly fry until soft ~ add parsley + dill. Cook a few minutes ~ add spinach, sea salt, mix. Turn off heat, add tofu, seasonings. Oil pans and roll out pie crust. Fill with cooled tofu filling. Cover with pie crust. Bake in hot oven till browned.

39

Millet Mushroom Stuffed Peppers

1 cup cooked millet
1 cube tofu ~ 6 oz.
1 cup sliced mushrooms
1 finely diced onion
¼ cup Good tasting yeast

mix with:

1½ teaspoon tarragon
½ teaspoon garlic powder
¼ teaspoon salt
2 tablespoons tamari
Pinch of thyme

mix ... Cut tops off peppers,
Stuff and bake ~
350° ~ 25 minutes
(cover)

Mushroom Tofu Fettucine

Prepare a pot of whole wheat or buckwheat noodles and set aside...

Sauté 1 cup mushrooms and scallions in 3 T. soybutter.
In blender combine: 12 oz. tofu
3 T. tamari
1 t. tarragon
2 T. lemon juice

Mix sautéd vegetables and sauce together and simmer on low heat for 10 minutes. Pour over noodles, sprinkle parsley on top and serve!

41

Rice Pancakes
with Tofu

(Serves 4)

2 cups cooked rice
2 cups mashed tofu
½ cup toasted, chopped walnuts
                    or pecans + raisins
2 T. lemon juice
1½ t. sea salt
★ Whole wheat flour to hold patties together.
★ Unrefined oil for frying

Mix ingredients (except oil) ~ form into
 small "patties"... Heat skillet, add oil
and fry until brown on one side.
Turn and brown the other side~

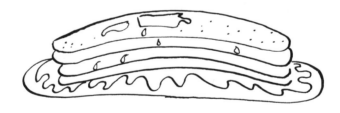

Tofu Saltim Boca

Slice large pieces of tofu (marinaded) and bread using tempura recipe –
Sauté in soy butter until golden brown ...

Put on a bed of spinach (lightly steamed) and rice.

Squeeze lemon over entire dish. Serve ~

PIZZA

Use whole wheat or pita bread
cut in half long way...
1 ripe tomatoe, sliced thin~
lay on top of bread.
Sprinkle with salt, garlic, basil
Take mashed tofu (12 ounces)
Add: 4 T. soy butter
       4 T. yeast flakes
       ¼ t. salt
       ¼ t. garlic powder
Mash well... top with
oregano + sliced mushrooms
Broil or bake until done!

Tofu Noodle Sauté

Prepare a pot of buckwheat
  noodles and set aside...

Brown tofu strips in sesame oil.
Take out of oil and blot. Sauté
chopped green pepper and onions.
Add sliced yellow squash or
zucchini.

   Place tofu in blender (10 oz.)
Add ¼ t. tarragon, ¼ t. garlic,
dash of pure water. Combine
noodles and vegetables and tofu.
Pour gravy over. Miso may be added.
Also sliced mushrooms.

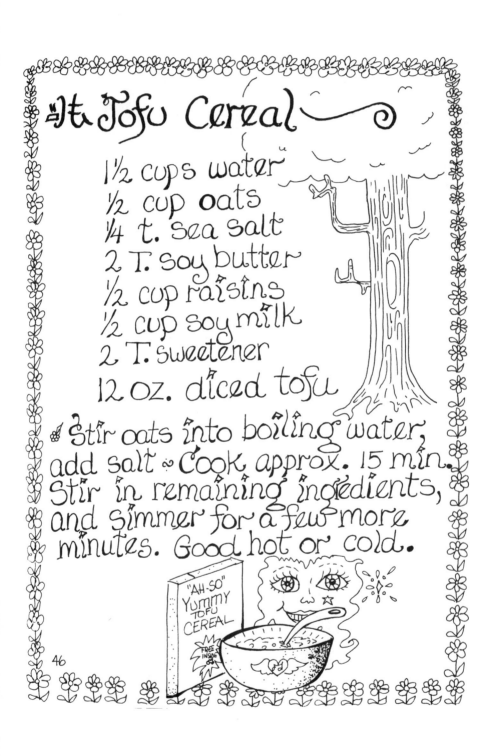

It. Tofu Cereal

1½ cups water
½ cup oats
¼ t. sea salt
2 T. soy butter
½ cup raisins
½ cup soy milk
2 T. sweetener
12 oz. diced tofu

Stir oats into boiling water, add salt ~ Cook approx. 15 min. Stir in remaining ingredients, and simmer for a few more minutes. Good hot or cold.

"AH-SO" Yummy TOFU CEREAL

FREE INSIDE

Thanksgiving Tofu Turkey

Help! SAVE ME!

This recipe will require your special effort, as you will have to make the tofu into a special mold. Follow tofu-making procedure ~ when you are ready to press use a large colander and lay cheese cloth inside and fill with curds. Press with plate. When firm, carefully remove and place in cold water. Refrigerate at least 1 hour before continuing...

Next:

Using a knife, hollow out a space for stuffing in bottom.

Use *favorite stuffing, and fill hole, gently ~ do not make hole too deep or wide!

Use pepper halves for "wings"

Pepper wings
CARROTS
stuffing

Use 2 carrots for "legs"

Carefully place pan over turkey and turn over...
Sauté onions with soybutter + umeboshi plums-opt., tamari.
Cover turkey with mixture ~
Cook slowly at 300° for about 40 minutes.
    Make a thick miso sauce with water, basil, celery seed.
Pour over while cooking.
Dust with primary yeast flakes.
To brown top, broil last few minutes.

★ Recipe given

Tofu Picnic

Using outdoor hibachi or grill, place marinaded slices of tofu on grill. Brown ~ serve with sauerkraut, mustard on sesame whole wheat buns. Sprouts, tomatoes, sliced onions & pickles make it a terrific picnic!

Tofu French Fries

Using a skillet or wok, heat sesame oil or any pure, healthy oil ~ Cut tofu in strips... Placing strips in hot oil. Be careful not to let the oil burn or smoke. Brown till all sides are golden in color. Drain on paper towel and sprinkle with sea salt or use tofu dip recipe given. Ketchup for the American traditional touch!

Country Bob's Baked Tofu

Use large pieces of tofu ~ Approximately 2 pounds for 5 people. Marinate 5 hours or overnight in one part tamari to three parts water, covering tofu. 1 T. lemon juice or rice vinegar, ½ t. dill, 1 t. grated ginger and garlic (opt.)

Place tofu on baking pan. Preheat oven to 350°. Pour ½ cup marinade in pan ~ bake 15 minutes.

Sauté 2 medium onions in soy margarine with ¼ t. ginger + 1 clove fresh garlic. Spread onions over top of tofu. Turn oven down to 275°. Baste continuously with liquid in pan every 10 minutes for 45 minutes.

Take 2 T. miso with warm water, enough to make a thin paste, and spoon over tofu. Turn oven to 200° for 5 minutes... Serve with brown rice...

50

Sloppy Song

1 whole large onion
1 stalk celery
3 tsp. sesame oil
10 oz. tofu
2 T. tamari
1 T. mustard
2 T. catsup or tomato sauce
1 chopped (pitted) umeboshi plum
1 T. miso

Heat oil in skillet. Chop onion and celery fine. Sauté until they are translucent. Squeeze out water from tofu and crumble into skillet. Sauté until golden brown. Add remaining ingredients. Stir fry for 5 minutes. Serve on pita bread with sprouts!

II. Tofu Salads

Tofu No~ Egg salad

20 ounces tofu
t. garlic powder
1 t. mustard (optional)
2 T. soy butter (or soy mayonnaise)
t. sea salt
t. lime juice
T. turmeric

Combine ingredients...
Turmeric makes the tofu
yellow~ like egg! Serve
on whole wheat bread
with lettuce and tomato
and mustard or mayonnaise.

Guacamole con tofu

Combine:

- 1 ripe avocado, mashed
- ½ chopped onion
- 1 chopped, ripe tomato
- 3 t. lemon juice
- 1 T. sea salt
- 1 clove crushed garlic
- 1 dash tabasco sauce
- 10 oz. diced tofu

Serve as a dip or spread.
*Okara is good mixed in, too!

54

Curried Tofu Rice Salad

16 oz. tofu in small pieces
2½ cups cooked, chilled brown rice
3 T. minced onion or leek
2 T. minced parsley
2 green peppers- one slivered-
    one sliced into rings
Dressing: 6 T. oil
            2 T. lemon juice
            1 t. curry powder
            ½ t. garlic powder
            3/4 t. salt

Combine first 4 ingredients with green pepper~ Add to dressing~ mix lightly, allow to stand a few hours.
Serve on lettuce leaves with tomato wedges & pepper rings. 55

Tofu ~ Waldorf Salad

Combine and mix well:

6 ounces tofu, drained + mashed well
½ cup grated carrots
½ cup diced apples
½ cup raisins
½ cup diced walnuts
1½ T. barley miso
1 t. sweetener
1 t. cider vinegar
2 T. Sesame butter

Serve on lettuce leaves, on toast... Great in Sandwiches!

III. Tofu In Soups

Miso~Vegetable Soup with Tofu

½ cup sliced scallions or onions
½ cup chopped celery
½ cup diced carrots
1 cube (6 oz.) tofu
½ cup sliced mushrooms
1 T. "Mugi" Miso

Heat sesame oil in pan. Add onions, cook a few minutes. Add all vegies, stir 2 minutes. Add 1 qt. water. Bring to boil-- cover--- simmer. Add crumbled tofu. Dill, parsley, basil may be added for flavor. To add Miso to soup ~ put miso paste in a cup, combine with soup stock. Blend well. Add to soup. Serve.

Love

Chinese~Bean Curd SOUP

1 cup sliced mushrooms
1 cup sliced leeks
Boil in a quart of water.
Add 1 piece of tofu sliced
in cubes. Boil 2 minutes.
Add 1 teaspoon salt
½ teaspoon dill weed.

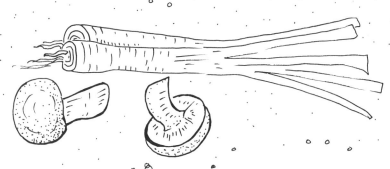

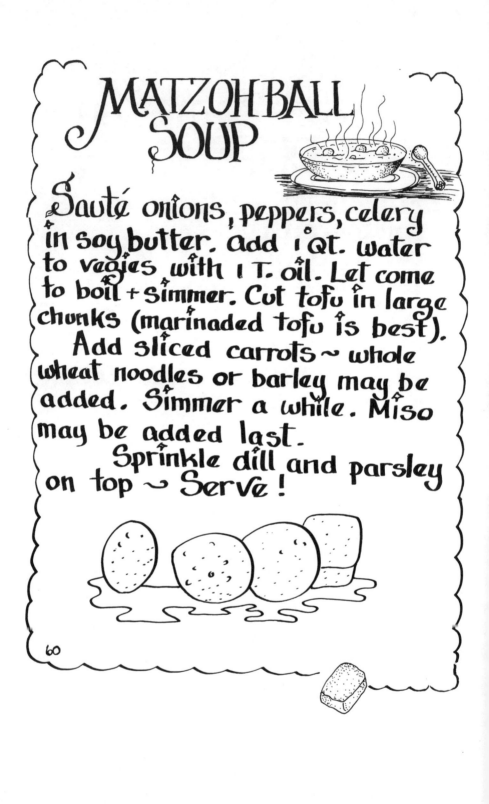

MATZOH BALL SOUP

Sauté onions, peppers, celery in soy butter. Add 1 Qt. water to vegies with 1 T. oil. Let come to boil + simmer. Cut tofu in large chunks (marinaded tofu is best).

Add sliced carrots ~ whole wheat noodles or barley may be added. Simmer a while. Miso may be added last.

Sprinkle dill and parsley on top ~ Serve!

60

IV. Tofu Desserts

Tofu Cheesecake

12 oz. tofu
1 T. vanilla
3 T. agar
1 cup Soymilk or juice
½ cup Sweetener

} Filling

☆ Crust~ Crumble graham crackers (Use enough to spread into pie pan) Mix with soy margarine and/or soy milk until slightly moist. Press into pan...

Heat soymilk and agar in pot until boiling. Simmer 2 minutes. Put tofu, vanilla + sweetener into blender. Add hot agar mixture, blend till smooth. (Add 1 T. carob powder if desired) Pour into pie crust~ chill until firm. Top with your favorite fruit!

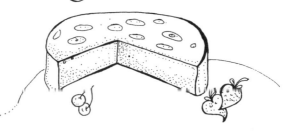

62

Pumpkin~Tofu Pie

❋ mix together in blender:
3¼ cup mashed pumpkin
1 cup soy milk
1 8 oz. cube of tofu
¼ cup arrowroot
¼ cup cashew butter
½ cup date sugar
1 T. vanilla
1 T. cinnamon
1½ T. molasses
½ t. salt

Pour into pie shell and bake at 425°
for 15 minutes, then at 250° for
1¼ hours. It will be firm when
cooled.

Millet~Tofu Pudding

1 cup cooked millet
1 cube mashed tofu (6 oz.)
¼ cup honey
¼ t. vanilla
Pinch ginger
¼ t. cinnamon
¼ cup raisins
⅛ cup chopped nuts

Mix together.

✳ oil baking dish. Cook 25 min.
(Sprinkle with kinako, nutmeg
and dot with soy butter.)

Tofu~Orange Custard Pie

(no ~ bake)

Use recipe for Tofu Cheesecake pie crust. "Soyola" can also be used to make a pie crust.

★ ★ ★ ★ ★ ★ ★ ★ ★ ★

Squeeze 2 cups orange juice into a pot. Add 2 T. agar-agar. Bring to a boil ~ simmer 3~5 minutes. Pour into blender.

Add: 1 T. Vanilla
      ¼ cup sweetener
      8 oz. tofu

Blend until smooth. Add peach or mango slices ~ Chill.

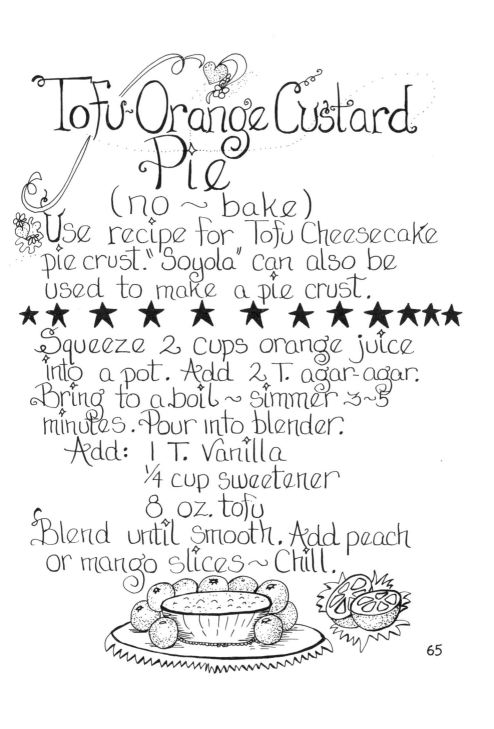

Easy Pie Crust !

2½ cups whole wheat or
        soy flour
⅓ cup water
⅔ cup coconut oil
1 t. salt

Sift flour and salt together.
Mix oil and water.
    Combine... stir lightly
with fork. Roll into ball.
Roll between waxed paper.
Place in pie pan and fill!

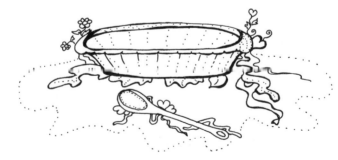

V. Okara Recipes

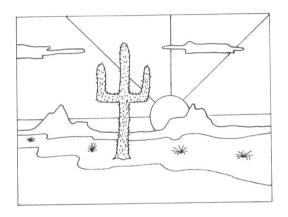

Soy Song Salad

Combine: 2 cups okara
½ green pepper ~ chopped
1 onion ~ minced
2 stalks celery ~ chopped
1 grated carrot

Dressing: ½ cup oil, 3 T. soy mayonnaise
¼ cup vinegar or lime juice.

Spices may be added ~ oregano, basil, dill, marjoram, thyme + garlic to taste. Combine ingredients, mix well. Top with roasted sunflower seeds ~ Makes a great sandwich with sprouts!

"Sabrosa"

Sauté chopped vegetables and
set aside...
  Prepare Miso dressing:
    2 T. oil
    3 T. miso
    4 T. vinegar
    3/4 T. sweetener
    1/2 T. kelp
    2 T. minced onion

Combine dressing with Okara
(soy pulp) mix together with
  sautéd vegetables... Form into
balls and roll in wheat germ.
    BAKE until hot...
* Or put into loaf pan ~ Add
  chopped nuts if desired!
Combine with rice for good hold-
      -ing power!

69

Sesame~Okara Cookies

Combine ~ 2 cups whole wheat flour
2 cups Okara
1 cup sesame seeds

Cream together and add to above mixture:

1 stick of soy butter
1 cup sweetener
4 t. baking soda
½ t. salt
1 t. vanilla
1 t. nutmeg
¼ cup raisins and/or nuts

Roll into balls and flatten slightly on greased cookie sheet. Bake for 20 minutes or until browned.

Okara~Fruit Delite

Pre-heat oven to 350°.
  Combine + mix well:
      2 cups okara
      ½ cup chopped walnuts
      1 cup soy milk
      ¼ cup molasses
      ¼ cup date pieces
      1 t. vanilla
      1 t. cinnamon
      1 t. nutmeg
      dash of salt
      3 tart apples in wedges
Spoon into lightly oiled casserole
dish and top with: ¼ cup "Soyola"
                    1 T. date sugar
                    ½ t. cinnamon

Bake 30 minutes or till
brown. *(add any other fruits
you like.)

SOYOLA

Pre-heat oven to 350°.

combine: 2 cups Okara
5 T. honey
4 T. date sugar
1/8 t. salt

mix well.

Spread on shallow pan. Roast in oven... till brown and crumbly. Stir occasionally.

*Add sesame seeds, raisins, wheat germ, shredded coconut, chopped walnuts, date pieces.

Favorite Stuffing

Sauté celery and onions in oil or soy butter, add sliced mushrooms. Sauté 5 minutes.

Add: 2 cups steamed chestnuts
2 cups cooked barley
2 cups bread crumbs
½ cup okara
1 T. SAGE
1 T. miso

Mix together adding water if needed. Great with tofu gravy ~ Use tofu sauce recipe adding chopped mushrooms, parsley and more tamari!

VI. Salad Dressings, Dips, Sauces and Creams

Green Goddess Avocado Dressing

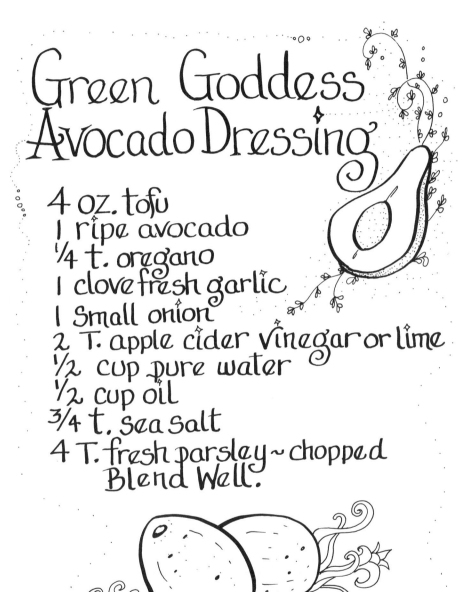

4 oz. tofu
1 ripe avocado
1/4 t. oregano
1 clove fresh garlic
1 small onion
2 T. apple cider vinegar or lime
1/2 cup pure water
1/2 cup oil
3/4 t. sea salt
4 T. fresh parsley ~ chopped
   Blend Well.

TOFU DIP~

2 oz. tamari
2 oz. pure water
Juice of one lemon
1 clove garlic
~Blend~

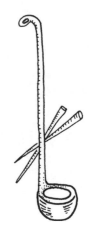

Thick Tofu Dip~

•Take above mixture and blend with one piece of tofu.

Tofu Mayonnaise

- 6 oz. tofu
- 3 T. lemon juice or vinegar
- 3 T. oil
- ½ t. salt ~ Blend well.

OR ~

~ Soy Milk Mayonnaise ~

1 cup cold soymilk in blender. Add slowly 2¼ cups oil. Fold in 1 T. sweetener; 1 T. vinegar, 1 t. salt.

(EGGLESS)

TOFU MAYO.

Tofu Marinade

combine:

> 2 cups water
> 4 T. soy sauce (tamari)
> ½ t. salt
> 4 pieces garlic
> 1 t. tarragon
> 2 t. vinegar
> 1 pinch thyme
> 1 t. dill weed

Place tofu in marinade~
refrigerate overnight.
(or longer)

Tofu Sauce

Put tofu in blender with a small amount of pure water.

Add tarragon & garlic.

Blend till creamy. Heat.
Add tamari to taste.
Serve over mushrooms, rice or
~ vegetables ~

Tofu Dressing

Combine sesame oil & lemon, oregano, garlic, tablespoon of honey, salt, dill, and 3 tablespoons of Tofu.
♡ Blend well. ♡

Tofu Sour Cream

1 cup tofu
juice of 1 lemon
½ to 1 teaspoon salt

Drop tofu into boiling salted water. Remove from heat and let sit 2 to 3 minutes. Squeeze out in your hands or cheesecloth to remove excess liquid. Place tofu in a blender, add lemon juice and salt. Blend until creamy and taste. If too sour, add more salt to counteract lemon.

Sweet Tofu Cream

(topping for Okara~fruit delite)

Pureé in blender:

    1 cup soymilk
    12 oz. Tofu
    3 T. molasses

Tofu Nut Butter

10 oz. tofu ~ mashed
6 T. nut butter ~ sesame, cashew or peanut
1 T. sweetener
1 t. lemon juice
1 T. miso or ½ t. salt

Blend well adding ¼ cup raisins and peanuts or sunflower seeds - chopped.

Tofu Whipped Cream

12 oz. tofu
3 T. sweetener
Dash of salt
1 T. Vanilla

Combine in blender until smooth. (For a yogurt-like flavor, reduce sweetener.)

VII. Soybeans & Milk & Tidbits ~

Kinako Kandy

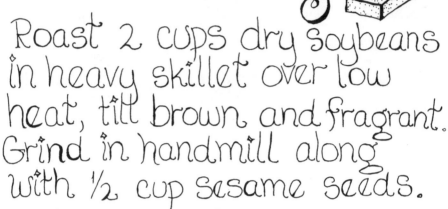

Roast 2 cups dry soybeans in heavy skillet over low heat, till brown and fragrant. Grind in handmill along with ½ cup sesame seeds.

Combine : 3 T. water
8 T. sweetener
4 T. date sugar
2 T. arrowroot

Simmer in saucepan over low heat till thick.

Mix soybean + sweetener mixture well. Press evenly in shallow pan. Chill for a few hours.

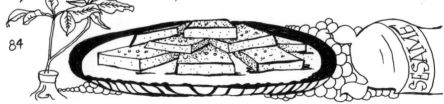

Soybean Candy Bar

Mix 2 cups date sugar with 2 cups sweetener...
Boil~
Add 1 cup roasted ground soybeans. Mix well. Top with sesame seeds and refrigerate ~

Hot Soymilk Cocoa

Heat 4 cups soymilk.
Add 5 T. Sweetener, 3 T. carob
Powder. Mix in blender.
Great on those cold mornings!

Frozen Tofu

If you have an excess amount of tofu, store it in the freezer. When you are ready to use it boil a pot of water, remove from heat, and place the frozen cube in the water. Let stand until completely thawed. Squeeze out excess water with paper towels in palms of hands. This tofu will be of a more fibrous consistency and may be used in any variety of ways.

Baby Food

Bananas + Tofu

Cut up ripe bananas, put in pan and heat. Add crumbled tofu and mix. This is good with Cream of Rice ~ Brown rice in oven and grind. Cook like cereal.

Pet Food

Okara is great for your pet! Mix with his favorite food. It contains 17% of the soybean protein and fiber (like bran).
Yeast, wheat germ, rice + avocado combined with Okara makes a healthy pet!

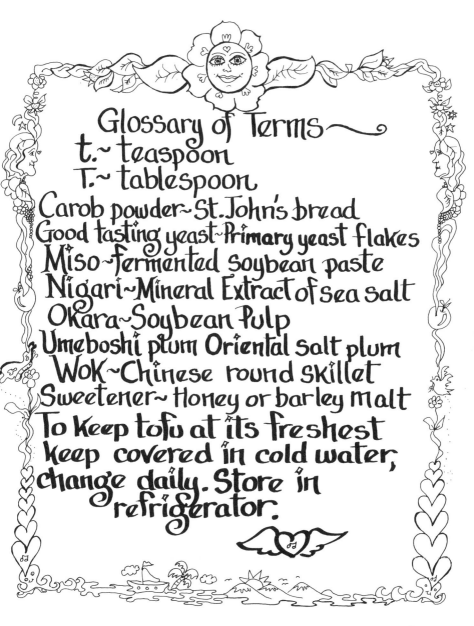

Glossary of Terms ~
t. ~ teaspoon
T. ~ tablespoon
Carob powder ~ St. John's bread
Good tasting yeast ~ Primary yeast flakes
Miso ~ fermented soybean paste
Nigari ~ Mineral Extract of sea salt
Okara ~ Soybean Pulp
Umeboshi plum Oriental salt plum
Wok ~ Chinese round skillet
Sweetener ~ Honey or barley malt
To keep tofu at its freshest
keep covered in cold water,
change daily. Store in
refrigerator.

Bibliography

William Shurtleff + Akiko Aoyagi, The Book of Tofu, by Autumn Press, Inc., 1975

Herman + Cornellia Aihara, Soybean Diet, George Ohsawa Macrobiotic Foundation, Inc., 1974

♡Special thanks to David Clisset, Cindy Blum, Don Eckard, Janet Baskin and Bill DeLaVega, Christine, Leon Rosenblatt for help in making this book whole.

♡Very Special thanks to my husband, Bob, who supplied me with all the tofu to discover all the recipes I could think of !

♡ Extra Special thanks from Bob and me to Bill Shurtleff and Akiko Aoyagi for spreading the light.

About the Authors

Bob Heartsong was born December 6, 1944, in Chicago, Illinois. He has been a vegetarian for a number of years, also studying yoga and meditation.

Toni Heartsong was born May 3, 1950, in New York City, N.Y. After her marriage to Bob, she became aware of the importance of a good diet and a healthy body.

Together they have devoted their lives to the communication of love and truth and helping others.